Stupid

Poems

9

Stupid Poems 9

Matador
9 Priory Business Park,
Wistow Road, Kibworth
Leicestershire LE8 0RX, UK
Tel: (+44) 116 2792299
Email: books@troubador.co.uk
Web: www.troubador.co.uk/matador

British Library Cataloguing in Publication Data.
A catalogue record for this book is available from the British Library.

ISBN 978 1780882 888

Typeset in 11pt Times New Roman by Troubador Publishing Ltd, Leicester, UK

Matador is an imprint of Troubador Publishing Ltd

Contents

Instructions for using this book   1

The Shostakovich final string quartet boogie   2

The average British person   4

A bad poem   5

The Law of Gravitation (or a poem with very long lines)   6

My social diary   7

A very silly poem   8

Poem by a performer in Cantus Arcticus   9

The church auction   10

Musical instruments eat in expensive restaurants   12

The hospital for very minor ailments   13

A story in which some words are spelled backwards   14

Shakespeare complains that his weekly rubbish collection
has been stopped   15

John Stuart Mill's primary school teacher talks to Mr.
and Mrs. at a parent-teacher meeting   16

Film actors and actresses do your housework   17

A Croydon Rhapsody   19

What shall we do with this round thing we've invented?   20

Poem about putting bags on your head   22

Anna Nicole   23

Lord Nelson suffered from seasickness   25

Fidelio   26

Useless pieces of advice   28

On the impossibility of making bubble and
squeak that doesn't have much squeak   29

The Lincolnshire mountain rescue team 30

A Midsummer Night's Dream 32

Poem inspired by an episode of The Simpsons 34

Duckworth-Lewis 35

Prince Igor 37

People in History with big beards (mostly men) 39

Why firework displays aren't much good on the radio 40

The Bartered Bride 41

Spurl 42

La Bohéme 43

Instructions for using this book

Press the button that's marked 'play',
And on the LED display…
This is nonsense, what I've said.
Please ignore what you've just read.
With thumb and finger grasp the edge
On the right side of the cover page.
Lift and open up the cover.
Underneath you will discover
That you've found another page.
Opening this won't take an age.
Repeat all this till you are able
Soon to see the contents table.
To choose a poem it is vital:
First of all to know its title.
Find the title on the list.
(You'll find this tricky if you're pissed).
They'll be a number right beside it
Which tells you on which page you'll find it.
Another way to use the book:
Just open up and take pot luck.
Or read it all from start to end.
When you've finished tell your friends.

The Shostakovich final string quartet boogie

Clap your hands and waggle your bum.
This piece of music is really glum.
It's the grimmest piece of music that there ever has been.
Shostakovich's string quartet number fifteen.

With a hey-diddle–diddle and a tiddle-pom-po.
It's got six movements and they're all real slow.
It's a good way for to finish your week.
Listen to this music that's really bleak.

Dance, dance, dance till you run out of energy.
The music begins with a movement that's an elegy.
And just when you're thinking that it can't get any sadder,
A funeral march follows not long later.

Play it loud so that your neighbours are annoyed.
Listen to the music and stare into the void.
You'll think that life is meaningless.
Listen to the music and get depressed.

This piece of music will never prove a
Pleasant background when pushing the Hoover.
On Radio 3 you might just get it.
On Classic FM you can forget it.

Dance, dance. dance till you're out of breath.
Listen to the music and think about death.
A bleaker piece of music you just can't get.
Shostakovich's fifteenth string quartet.

The average British person

The average British person likes a cup of tea.
The average British person enjoys a curry.
The average British person eats fried and boiled eggs.
The average British person has 1.99 legs.
The average British person has 2.3 kids.
The average British person does not exist.

A bad poem

This poem is well worth ignoring.
Turn the page; it's really boring.
As a narrative poem, it's no good.
It doesn't tell things as they should.
Nothing happens; no events.
This poem really makes no sense.
There are some lines that do not rhyme.
The poet doesn't make any effort to make it scan properly.
There is no subtle imagery.
No form or structure one can see.

A new verse starts for no reason.
There's no expression of emotion.
You must wonder what I meant.
It's a load of excrement.

The Law of Gravitation (or a poem with very long lines)

No-one knew why everything falls with the same
acceleration like Galileo said or why the Moon goes round
the Earth or all the bodies in space move as they do even
though they'd seen 'em,
Till Newton said that every particle attracts every other
particle with a force proportional to the product of their
masses and inversely proportional to the square of the
distance between 'em.

My social diary

Tomorrow I've an audience with the Pope.
He won't go on for too long I hope.
Then there's a reception at the Embassy.
These things seem to go on endlessly.
Dinner with the Beckhams – what a bore.
I've been there so many times before.
Then on Wednesday I'll receive a Nobel
Prize – I'll have to go, oh well.
Yet another garden party with the Queen.
I'll go there just to be seen.
Again, to the Palace I'm invited.
This time it is only to get knighted.
Sunday is the best day of the week.
On Sunday I will stay in bed and sleep.

A very silly poem

Criminals and grannies,
All the crooks and nannies,
Said: 'This is what the plan is:
We'll hide in nooks and crannies'.

Poem by a performer in Cantus Arcticus

(*Cantus Arcticus* is a fine, atmospheric piece of music by
Finnish composer Einojuhani Rautavaara. It is a 'concerto
for birds' - the orchestra accompanies a tape-recording of
bird calls.)

I'm not sure that my mating call
Should be heard by one and all.
It was really out of order;
This guy with a tape recorder
Comes along. I start to wonder:
'What's he doing in the Arctic tundra?'
I fly round in the Arctic mists.
Now I am a soloist
In a high class birdy song,
That is really not too long.
Anyone can listen to me,
If they buy the right CD.
The voices of the Arctic gloom
Can be heard in your front room.
If you listen you will learn:
You might have a nasty tern,
Screaming at you from your speakers.
It is a sound that is unique as
If you put your CD on,
You'll hear a migrating swan.

The church auction

Every priest
Costs at least
Twenty quid.
If you bid
Fifteen nicker
For a vicar,
You're no buyer.
It's even higher
For a bishop,
Or archbishop,
Which is why
A rabbi,
With his vestments,
Is an investment.
I would urge yer:
Get a verger,
Or be seekin'
For a deacon.
You cannot hope
To buy a pope.
An imam
Costs a leg and arm.

An ayatollah
Costs ninety dollar.
The same roughly
For a mufti.
But then who buys
Religious guys?

Musical instruments eat in expensive restaurants

Restaurants gone to by guitars
Have to have at least four stars.
If you dine out with a cello,
You must be a wealthy fellow.
You'll never see a violin
In a really vile inn.
The dearest food that you can get
Is eaten by a clarinet.
If you eat out with some trumpets,
You will not get just tea and crumpets.
You'll never get a saxophone
Bothering to eat at home.
Dinner, eaten by a gong,
Is at least five courses long.
The only food for a sitar:
The most expensive caviar.
Instruments, when they have their nosh,
Always go to somewhere posh.

The hospital for very minor ailments

You're sneezing a bit and have a slight chill.
You're not feeling good but aren't really ill.
You've a mild dose of flu or have a slight cold.
Under the weather or just growing old.
You've no need of major surgery,
Then this is the place where you should be.
A gentle bump has left a slight bruise;
This is the place that you should choose.
You've cut your finger and in need of a plaster;
You're bleeding a bit but it's no great disaster,
The nurses there are really fast
At applying a bit of Elastoplast.
You've twisted your ankle or stubbed your toe.
This is the place you really should go.
You've a bit of a headache; a mild hangover.
Just take a rest there until it is over.
This is where you should go along,
If there is really not much wrong.

A story in which some words are spelled backwards

He gets out of bed at eight kcolc'o.
It's Saturday so he's got no krow.
As he has breakfast there's a ring on the llebrood.
He gets up from the table and goes to the rood.
At the door, there stands the namtsop,
Who cheerfully greets him and hands him his tsop.
He goes through his post and picks out a rettel,
From a friend in the Middle East who works in the nonabeL,
Who's visiting England and landing at kciwtaG.
He goes to his car, which is in his egarag.
To meet his friend, he drives to the tropria.
He meets his friend when he gets off the tfarcria.
It's lunchtime now, so they go to a tnaruatser.
After lunch, it's time to tser.
He sits in a chair, and picks up a repapswen.
He does the crossword, and reads all the swen.
At six o'clock, it's time to tae.
He goes to the kitchen, and fixes his tea.
He makes some calls on the enohpelet,
And then spends his time watching noisivelet.
At eleven o'clock he goes to his moordeb.
It's been a tiring day so he goes straight to deb.

Shakespeare complains that his weekly rubbish collection has been stopped

I had a weekly collection but now they've taken that away.
I've complained about it, and so has Ann Hathaway.
I'm so mad about it; I'm rantin' and I'm ravin'.
You'd think they would do better in Stratford-on-Avon.
I can't be expected to write plays that are great,
When, to collect my rubbish, there's a fortnightly wait.
With rubbish piling up I find it really hard
If you wish, like me, to be the immortal bard.
It can't be expected that I can write a sonnet
With a great heap of garbage with vermin living on it.
I'm trying to write King Lear, Macbeth, Twelfth Night and Hamlet
In conditions that are unsanitory; it's really awful and it
Means I have to work with my legs knee-deep in litter.
I've recycled all I can, and I'm getting bitter.

John Stuart Mill's primary school teacher talks to Mr. and Mrs. Mill at a parent-teacher meeting

(the philosopher John Stuart Mill was learning Latin at
eight but didn't start learning Greek until he was ten)

'You've come about young Johnny Stuart.
He's good in Latin, almost fluent.
He is, however, rather weak
When it comes to learning Greek.
He's really good at Art and Craft,
But in Greek he is quite daft.
He's quite good when he does his sums,
And in P.E., but when it comes
To learning Greek, I don't know what'll
He do; he can't read Aristotle.
He masters well most of the basics.
He's a late developer in Classics.
He's really slow in Greek and that's
A problem when he does his SATS.
By now he should be taking home a
Book, or maybe two, by Homer,
And find it just as easy as
The complete works of Aeschylus.
Progress in Greek is really meagre.
He can't tell alpha from omega.'

Film actors and actresses do your housework

Marilyn Monroe and Diana Dors
Each take a turn at washing the floors.
Other good people for washing the floor
Are Mel Gibson and Demi Moore.
If you want the place tidy then Lawrence Olivier
Is really good at tidying stuff away.
If you have a clean house then Kenneth Branagh
Will make it look even spicker and spanner.
If you want the place tidy then get in George Clooney;
He'll speed about like a loony.
So your bedroom's a mess then what the heck.
Have it cleaned up by Gregory Peck.
There's nobody better at getting grime off than
Robert Redford or Dustin Hoffmann.
Judi Dench washes and Jeremy Irons.
Kevin Costner lights the fires.
Nicole Kidman makes beds, while Kate Winslet
Collects up the rubbish and then she bins it.
Always willing to take out the bin is
Peter O'Toole or Alec Guiness.
Michelle Pfeiffer dusts till Sigourney Weaver
Gives her a break when she comes to relieve 'er.

Simon Callow and Ian McKellen
Look after the dog and the cat really well 'n
The very best person for cleaning the loo is,
Without any question, Daniel Day-Lewis.
Susan Sarandon is really happy
At having to change the baby's nappy.
Then at the kids' bedtime Meryl Streep
Will read them a story to send them to sleep.
Your child must keep warm, so Charlton Heston
Will make sure in winter that he's put his vest on.
When making dinner then John Gielgud's
Favourite job is peeling spuds.
Brad Pitt chops onions and helps while John Cleese
Will lend a hand by shelling the peas.
Jamie Lee Curtis and Kevin Cline
Make a risotto that's really fine.
When doing your shopping there's nobody smarter
At saving money than Helena Bonham-Carter.
If you are thirsty then send out Tom Cruise
To the off-licence to get in some booze.
When he's not horrifying Christopher Lee
Does a nice job when making the tea.
If you want someone to boil up some water,
Just ask the Fondas: father and daughter.
If it's not working Liza Minelli
Is a dab hand at fixing the telly.
You can count on a star of the silver screen
To keep your house looking tidy and clean.

A Croydon Rhapsody

When I was young I was so fond all
Day of sitting by the Wandle,
And linger as the sun went down,
And darkness spread upon the town.
The very finest sight of all
Is sunset over Fairfield Hall.
Take me to your blocks of concrete.
Your underpass, your busy High Street.
This is the place that I'll be stopping.
In Whitgift Centre I'll go shopping.
This is the life that I would choose
Stuck all day in traffic queues.
The finest thing in all Creation
Is standing on East Croydon Station
As commuters make their way
Off to start their working day.
It is really such a lark
To run the dog in Lloyd Park.
If that's too far then what the heck?
We'll go instead to Park Hill Rec..
When sun goes down then I will hurry
To that little town in Surrey.

What shall we do with this round thing we've invented?

(In ancient Central America, the wheel was invented, but
put to no use other than as a toy)

Olmecs, Toltecs, Maya, Aztecs
Liked to walk around on their legs,
And although they had the wheel,
They said: 'This is how we feel:
We can't have cars to go around in.
We've no internal combustion engine.
We've things to put the rubbish in:
We've no use for the wheelie bin.
I s'pose we could invent the lorry,
But the fumes will make us sorry.
When we founded Tenochtitlan*
There was no traffic then on it and
If we had traffic jams, surely that'll
Greatly anger Quetzalcoatl**.
No word's for wheel when we chat all
Day and night in Nahuatl***.
Cars? We don't need them for
We walk or run on the M4****.
It has a useful function; it is
As a plaything for the kiddies'.

*Aztec capital city
**Aztec feathered-serpent god
***Aztec language
****Aztec motorway (not really)

Poem about putting bags on your head

Put a duffel
Bag on your noddle,
Or ensconce,
On your bonce,
A holdall, but,
On your nut,
There'd be weight
On your pate.
It's so zany and
On your cranium
You'd be merrier
With a carrier.

Anna Nicole

There's been Mimi and Isolde, Tosca and Carmen.
This is the story of the latest tragic heroine.
This contemporary opera does not concern the fate
Of someone in the distant past – it's right up to date.
With a jazzy score written by Mark-Anthony Turnage,
You might really enjoy it, if you don't mind bad language.
Anna Nicole Smith was a star of reality
TV – modern life in it's banality.
Anna Nicole was famous, just for being famous.
She had no special talent, apart from being famous.
Anna Nicole's short life was a modern tragedy,
And much of it on camera, and recorded for posterity.
She starts out in Mexia, a small town in Texas.
She has a dysfunctional family, and a flat chest as
She works in a fast-food joint, that serves up fried chicken.
She gets married and divorced, and is left with a kid and
Then she moves to Houston; she's hated Mexia for ages.
She works in the Wal-Mart, where she earns low wages.
She becomes a lap-dancer, and her earnings are bigger,
But is told that they'd be bigger still if she improved her figure.
So she has silicone implants, to enhance her bust,
But is left with chronic back-pain; take pain-killers she must.
('Do not fall for the convenient lie that beauty lies within.
This is just the hollow cry of those as ugly as sin'.)

She attracts the attention of Howard Marshall the Second:
Octogenarian billionaire, and soon they are wed and
She's got loads of money now; her life is full of parties,
But Howard Marshall dies (well, he is in his eighties).
She has a legal battle with his family for his money.
She is helped by Howard Stern, her lover and attorney.
('Money-grabbing, gold-digging, grave-robbing fake.
The story's really simple: hooker on the take.')
Her career goes from strength to strength through the next
few years.
In movies, on TV, and in *Playboy* she appears.
She gives birth to a baby live on pay-per-view TV.
(Tasteless though this seems to folk like you and me.)
Meanwhile, her mother is bringing up her son.
He dies from an overdose when visiting his mum.
He reaches for his camera, and takes a pic does Stern.
The only thing he's thought of is what they can earn.
Anna Nicole takes an overdose; she's decided to give up.
Of the culture of celebrity, she has had enough.

Lord Nelson suffered from seasickness

(true)

To beat the French is easy-peasy,
Even when I'm feeling queasy.
I was even seasick while
I fought the Battle of the Nile.
Even when I saw no ships,
My poor tummy had the yips.
I've one good eye that's for looking.
While at sea I'm mostly puking.
England expects each man to show up
And do his duty, while I throw up.
Kiss me Hardy – while you're on it,
I will try hard not to vomit.
I am even very, very
Seasick on the Woolwich ferry.
My Mum and Dad said to me:
I should never go to sea.

Fidelio

What's Beethoven's best opera? – asking this is fun,
For Ludwig van Beethoven only wrote the one.
This opera is a *singspiel* - there's lots of German chat,
But the music is so good you will put up with that.
The story is one of freedom from repression.
On the radical Beethoven it made a big impression.
Political prisoner Florestan is banged up in jail.
So loyal wife Leonore dresses as a male.
To get near to her husband she goes to the jail - oh!
She gets a job at the prison, and calls herself Fidelio.
Her disguise is so good Marzelline falls for her.
Marzelline is the daughter of Rocco, the jailor.
She is so keen on marrying Fidelio,
She rejects the advances of a real bloke: Jaquino.
The good-hearted Rocco lets the prisoners have a run,
As it's the birthday of the King and it's pleasant in the sun.
But all this effort to do a kind deed by Rocco
Earns only the wrath of nasty Governor Pizarro.
Now Pizarro is making plans to do in Florestan,
And makes Rocco and Fidelio dig a grave for the man.
But Fidelio says to Pizarro: 'Try and do your worst.
But if you kill Florestan, you'll have to kill me first'.
Now let's introduce Don Fernando, the minister,
Who thinks 'At the prison I suspect something sinister'.

His time at the nick comes in the nick of time.
For he sees what's been going on, and finds Pizarro's crime.
So Leonore is revealed as a heroine who's brave.
She's prepared to risk her life, her husband for to save.

Useless pieces of advice

(If you ring the BT Broadband Helpline because you can't get access to the Internet, you will hear a message telling you about a website you can visit to get help. Here are some more brilliantly unhelpful pieces of advice).

Your keys are inside and you've locked yourself out.
Just go inside and bring the keys out.
Your car will not start and you are in a panic.
Drive to a garage and get a mechanic.
You've misplaced your glasses somewhere in your room.
Put on your specs and you'll see them quite soon.
You're stuck overseas as your passport's misplaced.
Just go to England and get it replaced.
It's too dark to see where to put on the light.
With the light on you'll see it alright.
There isn't a problem that you can't solve,
If the problem's already solved.

On the impossibility of making bubble and squeak that doesn't have any squeak in it

You're a person quite unique,
If you like bubble but don't like squeak.
It's tough luck if you have a weakness
For eating bubble that is squeakless.
For if you ever try to seek
A plate of bubble that's got no squeak,
You will have a lot of trouble
In finding any squeak-free bubble.
So if you have for lunch today
Left over veg from yesterday
All fried together in the pan
Very soon you'll find you can
Not not have squeak mixed with your bubble.
It is quite impossible.

The Lincolnshire mountain rescue team

You'll never find people braver.
Always they're prepared to save a
Climber who's in trouble in
Lincs., where the air is thin.

They operate in Scunthorpe's
Lofty heights and Cleethorpes'
Icy crags and stony ways and
Rocky paths in Market Rasen.

They go out in the wind and snow.
Where there's danger; there they'll go.
They always show such fortitude
At fifty feet of altitude.

You're stranded on a gentle slope.
You have begun to give up hope.
You really don't know what to do.
They will come and rescue you.

They work in really wild places:
Windy heights and sheer rock-faces.
Let's hear it then; let's shout and scream
For Lincolnshire's mountain rescue team.

A Midsummer Night's Dream

This is a play by Shakespeare, who is our best-known
writer.
Theseus, Duke of Athens, will get wed to Hippolyta.
Hermia loves Lysander, and Lysander loves Hermia.
But Demetrius loves Hermia, and he is loved by Helena.
Fairy Queen and King: Titania and Oberon,
Just at the moment, really don't get on.
Peter Quince, the carpenter, and his 'rude mehanicals',
Rehearse *Pyramus and Thisbe* for amateur theatricals.
There's Bottom who's a weaver, and Starveling who's a
tailor,
Snug the joiner, Snout the tinker, Flute the bellows-
mender.
Oberon sends Puck to get a flower that's special.
Puck says: 'In forty minutes, round the Earth I'll put a
girdle'.
The juice from the flower, when dropped in someone's
eyes,
Makes her fall in love with the first thing she espies.
Oberon knows 'a bank, where the wild thyme blows.
Where oxlips, and the nodding violet grows'.
Et cetera, et cetera, and also that is where is
Sleeping Titania, Queen of all the fairies.

She's had some of the love-juice, and so the poor lass
Falls in love with Bottom, who has the head of an ass.
For Puck, full of mischief, has made Bottom go all wonky.
He's fitted Bottom out with the head of a donkey.
Puck, by mistake, gives some love-juice to Lysander,
Who, as a result, loves Helena and not Hermia.
Puck should have really dosed, not Lysander, but Demetrius.
And so he does this now, but it causes a lot of fuss.
Both Demetrius and Lysander say: 'I love you, miss'.
Helena thinks they're joking, and thinks they take the piss.
So the antidote is given to Lysander and Titania.
Lysander's back with Hermia, Demetrius is with Helena.
Now they can celebrate Theseus' wedding-day.
They get a good laugh when the mechanicals do their play.

Poem inspired by an episode of The Simpsons

(…in which Marge wonders why the baby is so quiet. The baby's quiet because Homer has taken the batteries out of the baby alarm to put into his remote-controlled model helicopter.)

The baby's lying in her cot.
But you do not care a jot.
Your helicopter keeps you happy,
But what about the baby's nappy?
For all we know the baby's crying.
You just want to keep it flying.
With the batteries in the handset,
The baby will get dirty and wet.
I really don't know why I bother.
You just want to make it hover.
What must really happen is:
You must get brand new batteries.

Duckworth-Lewis

(the Duckworth-Lewis method is the statistical method used
to recalculate how many runs are needed to win a limited-
over cricket match if time is lost due to rain. Nobody
understands it.)

A proposition by Wittgenstein,
Or the theory of Einstein,
Are just a piece of piss
Compared to Duckworth-Lewis.

I solve differential equations
On lots of occasions.
What I find hard to do is
The method of Duckworth-Lewis.

Clever people, like designers
Of large hadron colliders
Don't have to put up with
The method Lewis-Duckworth.

For hardness, learning Greek
Is really quite unique.
There's something harder: that's
Duckworth-Lewis' stats.

The best mathematicians,
The finest statisticians,
Apply their great big brains
To cricket when it rains.

Prince Igor

This opera by Borodin really isn't bad
For a chap who was a scientist and spent his time in the lab..
For Borodin's day job was organic chemistry.
Which has nothing at all to do with this old Russian story.
Putivl, I guess, is a town that's cold and frosty and
Prince Igor is going off to fight with the Polovtsians.
Going off to fight with him is Vladimir, his son.
Just before they leave there's an eclipse of the sun.
This is what happens just before they leave.
It is a bad omen, or so they all believe.
To his wife Yaroslavna, Igor says bye bye.
Yaroslavna is so scared for him, and fears that he might die.
Yaroslavna's brother Vladimir is left to mind the shop.
Bad idea, as Vladimir is a drunken slob.
(I'm afraid there are two characters, both called Vladimir.
One should be called Kevin, as confusion's what I fear).
Igor is captured by conquering king Khan Konchak.
Who says that 'I will treat you well; you do not have to go back'.
But Igor knows that saving Russia is really what he oughta
Do, though son Vladimir is in love with Konchak's daughter.
They're all entertained by the famed Dances Polovtsian.
The slave-girls all sing: 'We are slave-girls, what jolly fun'.
Meanwhile, back in Putivl, there's lots of bad behaviour.
Vladimir abducts a girl; Yaroslavna has to save 'er.

Christian Polovtsian Ovlour helps Igor to abscond.
He returns to Yaroslavna, of whom he is so fond.
Putivl is now open to Polovtsian attack.
But Igor has returned, and is ready to fight back.

People in History with big beards (mostly men)

All his mates said to Plato:
'We think your beard looks really great, oh!'
Charles Darwin's hairy chin
Used to have birds' nests in.
The long beard of George Bernard Shaw
Could hardly grow any more.
Brahms' sonatas for the 'cello
Were written by a hairy fellow.
Playing cricket, W.G. Grace
Used to have a hairy face.
A guy who was a real hoot in
The beard department was Rasputin.
Ivan the Terrible was greatly feared,
And he had a great big beard.
John Knox's friends said 'You oughta
Trim your beard so it is shorter'.
Nowadays a great long beard
Makes you look rather weird.

Why firework displays aren't much good on the radio

You will hear the bangs and whizzes,
The colours, though, are what one misses.
Radio fireworks are rather poxy,
Even if commentated by James Naughtie.
(This might have said Dimbleby,
But rhyming isn't simple, see.)
So when your radio is where at you are,
You will not see a show spectacular.
You will not see it; this is why
To see the rockets bursting in the sky,
If you want the display to see,
You'd better watch it on TV.

The Bartered Bride

Smetana's comic opera's a national institution if you're Czech.
The overture's terrific, and rattles on like heck.
Mařenka loves Jenik, and Jenik loves Mařenka.
They've not reckoned on Kecal, who is the marriage broker.
He's fixing up Mařenka with another, called Vašek,
Who is the son of Micha, and is a bit pathetic.
Kecal persuades Jenik to give up Mařenka and yield 'er
Provided she weds Micha's son and he gets 300 guilder.
So it seems that, for money, he's dropped her and forgot 'er.
When everybody hears of this, they all say 'What a rotter!'.
But Jenik's a long-lost son of Micha, and all along he's planned
To outwit Kecal, and win Mařenka's hand.
A circus comes to town, and with it Esmeralda.
Vašek takes a shine to her as soon as he's beheld 'er.
The circus needs someone to dress up like a bear.
Esmeralda persuades Vašek that the bear-suit he would wear.
Jenik's outwitted Kecal and Mařenka he has won,
And the opera ends with loads and loads of fun.

Spurl

Gimme an s, gimme a p, and give me a u.
Two letters left, we're almost through.
Give me an r, and give me an l.
What's that spell? What's that spell?
It spells 'spurl', which is a word
Of which you surely won't have heard.
You're wondering what meaning it has got.
The answer is: 'not a lot'.
But it's a word five letters long.
If you write 'sprul' you've spelt it wrong.
It has s at its head and l at its tail.
In this respect it's just like 'snail'.
In the dictionary it will fit
Before 'spurling' and after 'spurket'.
This poem is ending, sad to tell.
I must go off for a spurl.

La Bohème

This opera is so popular; if you wonder why,
I suppose that it is because it makes you want to cry.
Rodolfo lives in a flat with his artist chums.
They haven't got much money: they are a load of bums.
They're going to the café, to eat and drink in it.
Rodolfo says: 'Go on ahead, I'll join you in a minute'.
Mimi knocks on the door, she says she needs a light,
For her candle has gone out; we all think 'Yeah, right!'
Then she drops her key; they both look for it.
And he starts to sing about her tiny frozen mitt.
They fall in love at first sight, Rodolfo and Mimi,
But Mimi has a problem; as we'll see she has TB.
He says 'My mates are waiting now, at the café Momus.
I'm going off to meet them; I'd so love you to join us'.
They go off to the café, where the atmosphere is festive.
Rodolfo's friend Marcello has got rather restive.
For his old flame Musetta is there with an old geezer.
He suffers pangs of jealousy the minute that he sees 'er.
When the act ends she is back with Marcello,
And, left to pay the bill, is her poor old fellow.
The snowy city limits are the setting for Act 3.
Her relationship's not going well, or so says Mimi.
Rodolfo's insane jealousy is what she can't abide.
Rodolfo comes out, and he presents his side.

Mimi hides behind a tree as he gives his position.
What really concerns him is her medical condition.
When she overhears, the poor girl can't stop sobbing.
(And all in the audience also feel like blubbing.)
Mimi and Rodolfo have a heart-to-heart.
They decide that, for the moment, it is best to part.
Next we are in the flat, where we were for Act 1.
The four guys lark about; they are having fun.
They are interrupted by the arrival of Musetta.
Mimi is downstairs; they go down to get 'er.
The poor girl's on her last legs; she's coughing up like mad.
They do what they can, but the ending is so sad.

Lightning Source UK Ltd.
Milton Keynes UK
UKOW031926010812

196907UK00004B/16/P